D1426063

THE FELLOWSHIP OF THE SAINT

ALI HUSSAIN AL-RIDHA

authorHOUSE®

AuthorHouse™ UK
1663 Liberty Drive
Bloomington, IN 47403 USA
www.authorhouse.co.uk
Phone: 0800.197.4150

© *2018 Ali Hussain Al-Ridha. All rights reserved.*

No part of this book may be reproduced, stored in a retrieval system, or transmitted by any means without the written permission of the author.

Published by AuthorHouse 03/15/2018

ISBN: 978-1-5462-8690-5 (sc)
ISBN: 978-1-5462-8691-2 (hc)
ISBN: 978-1-5462-8689-9 (e)

Print information available on the last page.

Any people depicted in stock imagery provided by Getty Images are models, and such images are being used for illustrative purposes only.
Certain stock imagery © Getty Images.

This book is printed on acid-free paper.

Because of the dynamic nature of the Internet, any web addresses or links contained in this book may have changed since publication and may no longer be valid. The views expressed in this work are solely those of the author and do not necessarily reflect the views of the publisher, and the publisher hereby disclaims any responsibility for them.

Acknowledgements

I'd like to express my deep gratitude to my supervisor, Fayaz Ahmad, for his guidance, suggestions, and invaluable encouragement.

I'd also like foremost to thank my parents and wife for their endless love, trust, encouragement, and support throughout my life.

Finally, I would like to extend my sincere thanks and appreciation to all who have contributed in one way or another.

Biography

I first met Ali Hussain Al Ridha as an undergraduate student of English. I taught him for several years at Al Hasa Teachers' College in Saudi Arabia. As a student, Al Ridha impressed me as remarkably gifted with his genuine intellectual qualities. He always stood out among his peers for his seriousness of purpose, diligence and his constant desire to improve himself. Ali has excelled in academics but it has not dimmed his creative ardor and his love for writing fiction and poetry. What has struck me the most about Ali is the inventive and unconventional streak in his outlook that has always set him apart from others and spurred him on to seek new challenges.

Fayaz Ahmed

Centre for Preparatory Studies

Sultan Qaboos University

Muscat, Oman

Preface

Life is a chain of perceptions. It is human nature to seek answers. Therefore, I tried to put my thoughts in written words which bring together the profound and the prosaic, the mundane and the metaphysical, the simple and the philosophical in a beautiful synthesis. I also tried to suffuse my seemingly simple observations of life with such piercing insight and visionary passion that the experience of reading this book becomes a journey to the unknown. The content is not filled with dogmatic thoughts, so it serves universal spiritualism.

The book is composed of themes written in prose poems and delivered as spiritual sermons by a wise man called the Saint. He lives in abominable loneliness after the unfortunate departure of his beloved wife. He is about to unleash after years in isolation when the people of the village of Humbleton ask him to share his wisdom on the considerable matters of life, including passion, death, ambition, science, and marriage.

Some of the sentences in *The Fellowship of the Saint* will hopefully reverberate in your mind because of their dense meaning and epigrammatic brevity. They bear ample testimony to my lucid and powerful diction. Of course, some writings combine skilled craftsmanship with lyrical beauty. On the other hand, simplicity is the essence of some other writings.

Writing *The Fellowship of the Saint* was a truly rewarding experience. I am sure the readers will share my feelings when they read the book. It exudes conviction, sincerity, and honesty which certainly appeal to the serious reader looking for substance rather than instant gratification.

I wish you all the best.

High above a village called Humbleton, over a small lake, was built a solitary wooden cottage of a saint. The lake was shaded and surrounded by large, leafy-crowned willow trees. The scent of refreshing gardenia filled the air. The cottage was a real wonder to the beholder, and poetry emanated from every corner of its walls. A piece of Eden paradise, it was where sunshine turned its days into sweet imaginations, and moonlight turned its nights into divine weddings. It was indeed a masterpiece crafted with passion.

The Saint had great effect on people of the village. He was a dawn into the village. He changed people's minds and found new paths for them to approach. His own words elevated the spirit. But he lived in endless loneliness after his wife fell into the trap of sudden death, leaving a solitary man with no one to share the bitterness of earthly life. Loneliness was his constant shadow, his second self.

Loneliness dropped its shadow on the Saint's joyous countenances of the past. It also revealed to him the pages of his life tragedy. He read them with a gigantic will to cease the restless pulse of his afflicted heart, preventing him from viewing one's humble addition to humanity. Even the cottage turned from a haven to a slaughterhouse, where the Saint offered his heart and soul as a sacrifice.

The Saint suffered from the pangs of loneliness. He longed for connection like a thirsty deer quivering above a calm river guarded by the hungry crocodile of loneliness. It was a terrifying reality and made him empty within. A lonely sparrow he was. His wishes raced to find another sparrow with which he could share his joys and sorrows. Yes indeed, what is life without sharing?

The Saint could form no clear conception of the image of the hideous monster of loneliness. But it surely had torched his power of imagination to a great degree. He curiously pictured loneliness as a beautiful flower, opening to reveal its four petals and singing in a soft, hymn-like voice to seduce its victim. It kept its victim—him—trapped in a planet-like web and fed on his energy.

Then it uncovered its ugly face as a wizened, old, bald man. He had a thick moustache and a wide forehead with many lines. Each line told stories of its prey. His eagle eye was framed by thick brows. Such an image was certainly very unpleasant. Actually, it might be possible for such a man to be the elder son of Ezra.

It was a regular autumn day when the Saint felt an irresistible wave for connection. People of Humbleton always considered him an epitome of wisdom and spirituality. They needed to be preached to, so the Saint went to the temple, where the people of the village assembled when the sun of every Sunday rose high. It was a pleasant scene when they saw the Saint approach the temple. They stretched their arms in a warm welcome, with their tender hands folded in need.

The Saint descended the few steps of the temple. Every step sounded like a melody whose echo penetrated the still air. A halo of virtuosity grew around him as he stretched his arms forward. He gazed in eagerness at people with those eyes framed by thick, silver-white eyebrows. With a voice that seemed like the roar of a great ocean, he preached,

> O people of Humbleton village,
> Let those who have an eye and an ear
> See and hear.

> God never fails to reward
> People of righteous deeds

And were patient to life's burdens.

Such a life has nothing

They desire besides God.

By desire, they shall be driven

To the kingdom of God,

To well-watered gardens

A foot never set.

Rivers of milk and honey,

Beneath shall be flown.

Impossible

To describe in words.

Severely punished,

Those who took misleaders as helpers.

Diseased were their hearts.

Locked were their minds.

By desire, they shall be driven

To the valley of hell shadows.

Impossible

To describe in words.

In wonder, misbelievers look

To your creature,

Forgetting on purpose
God is the wonderer.

Have fear!
Associate not with God.
Resurrected all of you shall be
On the day of the great panic.

Believe not!
The hour of resurrection
Will never come.
Not to be doubted.
Surely overtake you suddenly.
To God we all shall be
Indeed gathered and returned.
A day when all people
Shall become like moths.

I will lift my hands
In your name, my God.

Upon you alone I will call.
Your servant may

Seek stairs to heaven.
The disobedient may
Seek a path to hell.

The Saint sat on a threshold. A creaky sound came from his wizened legs that could not support his feeble body without leaning on a walking cane. People gathered closely around him. He said,

I came to say a word,
Not of my experience,
But of my lovingness and faith.

And not in vain I shall speak
Until the truth reveals itself in a greater voice,
And the mist of your eyes shall turn to be the mist of your hearts.
Never need to be ashamed of your queries
For they are rain
Upon the land of ignorance.

People of Humbleton showered the Saint with questions from which curiosity emanated. Their deep hunger snatched the Saint from the claws of loneliness. Yet his breath recites the hymn of his tragedy.

A man said, 'Speak to us of the unknown.'

The Saint raised his head, and there fell a great silence upon everyone. With a greater voice, the Saint said,

> We are neither able nor willing to seek
> the gate of the unknown
> Save with the hand of the Almighty.
> When we feel curious,
> We pursue it as an aim in itself and not as
> a means to achieve certain ends.
> If we show exaltation before the
> elevation,
> We consider it a form of penalty.
> If we yearn for something,
> We regard yearning a blessing in itself.

We also know that the furthest matters
Are the most worthy of our tendencies.

What is it
To open the gate of the unknown
But to be free from the shackles of life?
And what is it
To break the shackles of life
But to dwell and sail in the soul of life?
Then you shall indeed
Unveil and delve into the unknown.

Answers are besieged in the depths
Of your thoughts, dreams, and hopes.
Open the home of your memories wide.

On the way of infinite musings,
You shall witness the autumn
Of silent knowledge.

Only with the beginning of another life
Will you live.
Satisfaction shall no more be found

Until your body turns to dust and ash.

In truth,

We are capable of finding the key to the
unknown

In the smallest gestures of the spirit.

In a simple drop of dew.

We might find all the beauty and
creativity

In the smile of an infant.

We can see all the faith, aspiration, and
hope of humankind.

Knowing the Saint was afflicted with loneliness, a middle-aged woman said,

Speak to us of loneliness.

The Saint's eyes were soaked with tears of great sadness.
He spoke with veiled words, saying,

Today
I stand alone.
A look of pain crosses my face
As I drink my misery.

Swept
By the waves of loneliness.

Ali Hussain Al-Ridha

Slices of memories scatter
As fragments of a broken mirror.

What am I except
An echo of a forgotten poem,
Desperate for connection?

Then a scholar asked, 'What of knowledge, Master?'

And the Saint answered,

> Knowledge is breaking the shell of
> ignorance
> That encloses the distance
> To the dawn of understanding.

> Knowledge is the crutch for the human
> When the behemoth of life's burdens
> Bows down one's backbone.
> For knowledge weaves a net of solutions
> Which radiate the secret path
> Through which you can catch the elusive
> cart of earthly bounty.

All knowledge is vain save when there is
an action.
All actions are empty save when there is
passion.

Yet
Knowledge cannot break
The constant presence of two things:
Foolishness of humanity
And the prison-house of destiny.

Remember...
There is no scale that can weigh your
intellectual needs.
Let the sky be your limit.

Then a sinner asked, 'What of the past?'

A sob came from the Saint's throat. Then he answered,

> Long were the days of past.
> You have lived
> Within its silent walls.
> And long were the nights of torment.
>
> Who can draw oneself apart
> From the past without regret and sorrow?
>
> And who can start again
> As a blank sheet
> In the book of existence?

Ali Hussain Al-Ridha

The past is not a thought

You wash away

But a memory,

Graven for eternity.

Nor it is an event to disappear

In the pages of history.

But a phoenix always rises from its ashes.

Then the sinner spoke again and asked, 'What of conscience?'

The Saint replied,

> The conscience of goodness
> accompanies us
> Since our births, as well as the
> consciousness of absolute destruction.

> But it will remain the true justice of life
> Which will judge you,
> Protect you when you are innocent,
> Deny you when you are guilty.

> Consciousness knows no fear of earthly
> matters and accepts no warning of beasts.

Then a young man said, 'Speak to us of dreams and ambition.'

And the Saint answered,

Your dreams are your other self,
Dwelling beyond the border of reality.
They conceal much of your desires.

Your mind tends to interpret them.
Your heart tends to love them.
Your soul tends to fulfil them.

Ask not, fool, who doesn't sell one's
dreams for fortune?
But ask, fool, who deems that dreams are
weighable?
Dream is the true house of fortune,

Destroyed by the thieves of greed.

Say not the dreamer remains half-asleep
In the fruit of ignorance.
But say the dreamer remains half-awake
In the dawn of ambition.

Dreams teach you the way of ambition
Which awakens you by its fire.

Therefore,
Seek ever to embrace the torch of
ambition.
Failure does not mean your inability to
achieve your goal.
It means living without ambition.

Then a family man said, 'Speak to us of marriage, Master.'

With a smile coursing up his cheeks, he answered,

> Marriage is the sacred union of two
> divine souls
> So they become great companions,
>
> Who console the other
> When burdens of life are multiplied.
>
> Who relieve the other
> When cares become heavy upon his or
> her shoulders.

Then a man spoke loudly. 'Speak to us of pessimism and optimism.'

And the Saint said to him,

> Pessimism is walking the rough
> path of life
> Loaded with the shackles of dark visions.

> It could never find an outlet to the world
> Of success and happiness
> Because of slim hope,
> Withering between great despair and
> deep sorrow.

> Until optimism comes
> To open the heart's gates and light its
> corners,

Surmounting the obstacles of pessimism.
Let there be no scale
To measure your optimism
And wave around your heart
A net of infinite hope.
Hope is the vision of nobility and
goodness
Amid pervasive evil and misery of life.

Forget not.
Look up to behold the sunlight.
Never look down to behold the shadow.

Then a rich man asked, 'What of greed and contentment, Master?'

The Saint answered,

> Greed is a battle fought
> In your epic fantasy,
> And desires are the rattling of bones.

> It leads people like a flock of lambs
> To the slaughterhouse.

> God bestowed upon your soul
> Contentment and earthly satisfaction
> That would desert you and vanish forever
> On the first sigh of greed.

Let contentment be
An echo, racing with your breath.
Music of eternity goes in exact harmony
With your spirit's desires.

Sometimes,
God takes from us everything
To teach us the value of everything.

Then a feeble man said, 'Speak to us of death.'

The Saint spoke, saying,

> You might unveil the mystery of death,
> But how would you reach it unless
> you seek
> In the heart of life and embrace all its
> secrets?
>
> The bat which is indeed
> The ambassador of darkness
> Cannot unveil
> The enigmatic power of light.
>
> If you would indeed dwell in the seed of
> death,
> Be a poet whose soul quivers in rhythm

With fragments of life.

Yet

I have come to the terrifying conclusion

I will always remain a prisoner

In the cage of my curiosity.

Life is a sphere.

What am I except a fragment abandoned

In the corner of my own understanding?

The rich man spoke again and asked, 'What of satisfaction?'

He answered,

> How odd!
> I can get no more satisfaction.
>
> Such greed,
> Seeded and watered by envy,
> Changed my heart to a stone.
> Changed my ambition to a cold fire.
> Left me without dignity or friends.
>
> Yet
> I can get no more satisfaction.
>
> A mortal jot it really is,

Seeks heavenly pleasure
An earthly creature would never
experience.
I cannot change this truth.

Yet
I can get no more satisfaction.

Then a generous man said, 'Speak to us of giving, Master.'

The answered him.

Giving!

The source of sincere love,
The spring of inner light and fortune,
The well of sacred water,
The blessing of old age!

Indeed,
The dawn of a brighter tomorrow
through its warmness.

Your giving can dry tears of humanity
And its taunting poverty.

Giving creates a noble caravan,
Pursuing the world of spirit elevation
Which might be lost.
For the rough path leading to the
carpeted ground with white jasmine is
Never free of ambushes and deceivers.

Then a woman asked, 'What of liberation?'

He answered her,

> Because of our ignorance,
> We appear to be finite.
> Knowledge might be the certain cause for
> liberation.
> Action by itself
> Cannot destroy our illusions.
>
> Knowledge helps self reveal itself by
> itself,
> Like the sun when the clouds are
> removed.

Of course,
God made knowledge with many windows
To satisfy every scholar who looks
through.

Then a man who lost his faith in justice
Spoke and asked, 'What of revenge, Master?'

And the Saint answered, saying,

> An ugly appearance of justice,
> Walking asleep
> In the mist.
>
> Looking for its own right,
> Bathing and anointing itself
> With the blood of its victims.
>
> Assuming punishment is itself justified.

Then a child who was abused said, 'Speak to us of cruelty, Master.'

A look of sadness crossed the Saint's face as he answered.

An ugly scream,
Trodden deeper and deeper
In a bath of tears,
Takes you from
The warm cradle of humanity
To the cold grave of savagery.
Changes you from
An instrument of inspiration
To a tool of torment.

Then a woman who adores her beauty said,
'Speak to us of beauty.'

And he answered her,

> Behold the mirror!
> Tell me what you see.
> A feeble woman adores her mortal
> beauty,
> Wishing a beautiful rose
> Shall ever live young.
> Have not you known?
> Buried would be the beauty.
> Snowed would be its rose,
> Abandoned in the corner
> Of the past.

Then a religious man asked, 'What of praying and fasting, Master?'

The Saint answered,

> Praying is a matter of the heart.
> It lies in the realm of feeling and intuition
> to reach the serenity of one's soul.
>
> Fasting is like a tree in which
> Worship is its roots,
> Patience is its trunk,
> And the other moralities are its branches.
> Forget not that.
> Praying and fasting together become
> Your spirit brides,
> Appearing as in the ceremonial custom
> Of al-Qader night.

Then a flower girl asked, 'What of the flowers, Master?'

And he answered her,

> It is the bride
> Who was sent by our Mother Nature
> To inspire humanity
> And excite the world.
> Conceived in the womb of winter,
> Was born in spring, Reared in the bosom
> of summer, and Slept in the bed of
> autumn.

> In other words,
> It is a secret of heaven
> Unveiled to earth.

Then a wizened old woman who lost her son in the war said, 'Speak to us of war, Master.'

And he said to her,

> An epic mosaic
> Embodies
> All complexities of human beings—
> Of hate, grudge, and greed.
> That is war.

> I called and called
> In the dark,
> Trying to find a reason for wars.

> Stillness made me cry.
> Pain made me bleed tears.

Ali Hussain Al-Ridha

My beloved, I am tired.
We want our sons back.

Why cannot they return?
Waiting for hope.
Waiting for peace.
Waiting for an opportunity to say
In a loud voice...

'Goodbye, cruel world.'

Then a man asked, 'What does paradise look like?'

The Saint answered,

> In the depth of life,
> A poem I shall hear
> With no words.
>
> Melting with my soul,
> Dancing,
> Walking in the clouds,
> Living in the paradise
> Of my imagination.
>
> You have your paradise,
> And I have mine.

Then a lover said, 'Speak to us of passion and reality.'

The Saint answered him, saying,

> Life is not just a journey devoid of
> passion.
> Passion forms the core of our existence.
>
> Passion is an enduring source of
> sustenance
> For the mind as well as the heart.
>
> Yet
> Much of my heart remains unsaid.
> Only if my passion could fly higher than
> reality.

Ali Hussain Al-Ridha

My spirit shall wander upon the twilight,
Between the darkness of my desire
And the light of my faith.

My thoughts shall sail beyond illusion to
reach
The realm of fantasy.

My body would float in the mist of every
dawn.

Only if my passion could fly higher than
reality.

Then a philosopher said to the Saint, 'Speak about the dual nature of humanity.'

And the Saint answered,

> Sometimes,
> In the shore of your self-pygmy,
> The dark calls you
> To drain the bitter potion,
> And you must embark.

> Some other times,
> In the shore of your self-God,
> Your sacred spirit calls you
> To be the flute through which
> Life breathes the melody of virtue.

> Behold yourself!

Ali Hussain Al-Ridha

A prisoner
In the twilight of duality
Between
Your self-God and self-pygmy.

Then a man said, 'Speak to us of yesterday, today, and tomorrow.'

And he answered,

I must ask...

Does today carry the regrets of our pasts
And the worries of our futures?
Or does it embrace the memories of the
past
And the hopes of the future?

Yet
I have found no answers.

A seeker of truth asked, 'How can I reach the truth?'

And the Saint replied,

> A seeker of truth am I,
> And what treasure have I found in truth
> Which I may reap after bitter patience?
>
> Or a tunnel of truth am I,
> That the hand of the Lord may use
> To emerge the light at the end of the tunnel.
>
> That is the question.
>
> No one reveals the truth
> But may reach its threshold.

The narrator may narrate the story
Yet cannot give you the eye which
captures the scene
Nor the moment that touches your heart.

Truth enfolds itself like a spike of
countless flowers.

Say not I have revealed the truth,
But say I have breathed from the sphere
of truth
And found a leaf from its heavily
laden-tree.

For the truth is like a vast ocean,
Where the individual infinitely pursues
its depth
Yet will ever barely touch its surface.

Then a poor man asked, 'How can I live in this world?'

The Saint answered,

> In a world that demands perfection
> Death might be easy because life is
> difficult.

> The course of life never runs smoothly.
> The poor has no remedy but only faith,
> Though well seems to be the second
> torch to qualify.

Then a religious woman asked, 'What of spirit elevation?'

He answered, saying,

> Only when your soul
> Walks, roaming
> Upon the moonlight,
> Alone you commit a sin.
> The soul shall fly, singing
> Upon the wind,
> When lust withers in the dark.

Then, a nurse said, 'Speak to us of grace, Master.'

He answered,

> Grace is when God gives us
> Relief whenever there is pain,
> Serenity wherever there is fear, and
> Acceptance whenever the end is near.
>
> Angels have a supreme fondness for grace
> For it bestows majesty and serenity
> within a person's spirit.

Then the philosopher spoke again and asked,
'Does God exist?'

And the Saint answered,

> There is no God
> In the absence of observation.
> Observation creates reality.
> Yet
> We know everything
> Only when we recognize
> Its first cause and principle.
> For God is a thought
> To be among the causes of all matters
> And to be the first principle.

Then a narcissist asked, 'What of narcissism?'

And he answered,

> Narcissism is dissolving in love.
> As an extreme form of egotism and
> karma.
> It is the realm of fantasy and
> self-delusion.
>
> Sometimes,
> Narcissism is the twin sister of
> selfishness.

A dying man said, 'Tell us about the strong and the weak.'

The Saint answered him,

> Of the strong and the weak, in you I can
> speak
> For what is weak but strong in need.
> You are strong when you are with God.
> You are weak when you are not
> with God.
>
> For a ranger without a campus
> May roam among fatal wilderness.
>
> Even pain may strengthen the weak
> whose string is rooted to God

For it draws us apart from our worldly
lust
And draws us close to God.
God knows we need never be ashamed of
our weaknesses
For they are the rain upon our overlying
seeds,
Hidden in the heart of self-righteousness.

Yet beware of the elusive steps of your
worldly lust.
You are besieged in a perilous battlefield
Upon which your worldly lust wages war
against your mind.

Let God's judgement and reason be your
peacemaker
Who translates the conflict of your
elements into harmony.

Then a man spoke and asked, 'What of musing, Master?'

And the Saint replied,

> Musing is walking in the shadow
> Of the temple towards
> The sacred path of life
> As a step from the known to the
> unknown.

> It is also a short approach to
> The threshold of infinite knowledge.

> Musing is like an ocean,
> Always much more to see in the depths
> than its surface.

But few are the divers who seek the
treasures hidden below.

Musing is the opening and closing of a
window,
Leaving those baffled beholders to guess
About what is seen during the moment.
Perhaps they draw images powerful
enough
To capture a fraction of this vast universe.

Then the same man spoke again and asked,
'Would you speak of peace, Master?'

The Saint answered him, saying,

> The symbol of love and joy
> For its magic meaning is a soft bed
> Upon which your soul rests.
>
> Until she becomes flooded
> With an ocean of serenity.
>
> And the hands of oblivion
> Are deeply engulfing humanity.

Then the sheriff of the village said, 'Speak to us of politics, please.'

He answered,

> Politics is a false matter
> Driven by shrewdness,
> Used to rationalize immoral decisions.
>
> Ties you with chains of earthly authority
> With a strange mixture of crabbed
> tenderness
> And shrewd understanding.

Then a man afflicted with doubt asked, 'What of doubt, Master?'

And he said to him,

> Doubt cloaks you in the shadow of
> confusion
> To fall into the trap of delusion.
>
> Leaving you moving in a vicious circle,
> Like a blind rat groping out of the maze.
>
> And doubt stands with observing eyes
> To witness your drama.

Then a nun said, 'Speak to us of hypocrisy.'

The Saint said to her,

> A disgusting mask,
> Concealing the ugliness of detestation
> Beyond the outer garment of love.
>
> Could be both
> A name of need and a symptom of
> disease.
>
> Therefore,
> Innocence is the daughter of faith,
>
> Who keeps guards over a person's soul.

Then a widow asked, 'What about yearning?'

With a tear dropping down his cheek as he remembered the tragic departure of his wife, the Saint answered,

Yearning is a wave from our yesterdays,
Mirroring a passing flock of sealed memories
To cease the journey in the gulf of forgetfulness.

Too many memories have my wife scattered in my soul,
And too many are of the laughter she seeded in my dreams.

How often have I

Crawled into her pillow, looking for
warmth

Until my yearning melted into a running
brook,

Flowing in the lake of silence.

Then a man asked, 'What of the unity of humanity, Master?'

And he answered,

> Say not humanity is in my heart,
> But say I am in the heart of humanity
> Because we are one nation,
> One tribe,
> One race,
> One colour,
> One language,
> One religion,
> One belief.
> We are indeed Adam's sons
> And daughters despite our differences.

After the sun withdrew its rays from the horizon, the high tide of night swallowed the village. The entire village was bathed in the soft blanket of moonlight, and a tremendous stillness descended. The Saint said,

> The dark bids me leave you.
> But the hour of our departure
> Shall be the hour of our souls' gathering.
>
> Though painful absence and bitter
> patience
> Might enfold my remembrance,
> My love-tide will visit your souls
> To breathe life into the barren shores
> Of your sweetest dreams
> And quench your eager minds.
>
> May God bless your souls that listened
> to me.
> Now let's all raise our hands and plead
> with the Almighty.

O heavenly Lord, hear our prayers.
I beg, your majesty, question me no
further of my sins,
And let little drops of pity fall for us who
have committed sins.

Exalted your name shall be
On your earth as it is in your paradise.
Your will shall prevail.
In your name, we shall believe.

God is the Almighty, bringing to
nothingness
The understanding of a wise individual.
One does not need to shout to be heard.

For people who love him,
For people who fear him—young and
great—
For people in whom he is well pleased.

No eye has seen, nor has an ear heard,
Things God prepared for those.

Blessed are those who are hungry shall
be full.
Blessed are those who are poor shall be
rich.
Blessed are those who are weeping shall
be laughing.

For those whose ears are hard of hearing.
For those whose eyes are closed.
For those whose hearts have grown dull.
For those who knew the truth and
turned away.

Misery and perdition are in their way.
Comfort and peace they will never reach.
Hark!
Those who are full shall be hungry.
Those who are rich shall be poor.
Those who are laughing shall be
weeping.

At least they should hear and understand,
At least they should see and think,

So God would guide them to the path of
enlightenment.

If your hand guides you to commit a sin,
Cut it.
It is better to be in paradise with one
hand
Than being in hell with two.

Amen!

Just before the Saint left, the religious man said,

Let not the pangs of loneliness
separate us,
Nor the moments you have spent with us
Become a memory we treasure.
Neither stranger nor guest you are
But a father and our beloved,
And much have we loved you.
But speechless our love was.

We shall remember you as a generous
philosopher,

Who left us with a deep ocean of
thoughts
That you scattered like succulent petals of
roses.
But forgetfulness might blow these petals
To the depth of its valley.
We shall remember you as the wayfarer,
Who remembers the green prairies
In which his image was reflected as he
drank
From its sweet brook.
But your memory may take us eventually
On the wings of the last chapter of our
story.

The Saint walked among them an angel, and his
words were a light upon their souls. Too many
words did the Saint scatter in these people, but
deep was their thirst. Their needs could never
bind him. Nor does their love hold him. Their
endless queries were as a lily buried beneath

snow, dreaming of spring. Yet strangely, hope shall ever remain their comforting groom.

The Saint walked with the hasty wind, seeking his cottage. He heard a curious murmuring sound, so he stood still and lifted his face towards the sky. He saw a swallow, singing and sailing with Nissan's breeze. The swallow made the Saint remember his wife with grief. In a crying voice which seemed like a wounded lion and heavy tears wetting his feeble cheeks, the Saint called his departed wife, saying,

> O swallow,
> My little swallow,
> Come
> From the garden of paradise.
> Meet my eternal yearning.

> O swallow,
> My little swallow,
> Sing.
> Let your melody

Echo verses from
The temple of love.

O swallow,
My little swallow,
The winter is never too cold
With your warm memory.

O swallow,
My little swallow,
Have mercy!
I need your love.
Twitter in the sky.
A heavenly ecstasy it truly is.
It shall satisfy
My exalted ego.

O swallow,
My little swallow,
Open your golden wings
Upon your passionate chest.
Hug me.
Feel my pulse.

Be my companion.

O swallow,
My little swallow,
Come
From the garden of paradise.
Meet my eternal yearning.

The Saint always knew it is much easier to drain the bitter potion of life and fall victim to the clutches of loneliness than to accept destiny's will that is the certain path to serenity, happiness, and spiritual peace. If her remembrance comforts him, let him be ever lonely. He tirelessly walked the mystic mile under the grey sky of loneliness.

The Saint reached his cottage, where he ended another day. He opened the old door so slowly that roamers could hear the echo of its hinges squeaking in unison with the moaning of the Saint, who left the old door opening like the mouth of a feeble, yawning mammoth. He closed his eyes, wishing his wife to be awakened from the deep swoon of death. But his wishes only brought a slim hope which withered between bitter reality and horrible despair. Perhaps the seeds of the Saint's mute ordeal grew in silence and deadened him away.

The Saint heard the wind whistle through willow trees. There begun to appear among trees a bald head followed by a wide forehead, and then thick brows and a moustache. These facial features were more than enough for the Saint to recognize the elder son of Ezra, who strode towards the Saint and took his soul like a moustachioed eagle dragging a young gazelle with his sharpened claws.

The Saint instinctively tried to escape, but he felt feeble. It was a smashing defeat for him. There was feverish triumph in the bald man's eyes and a wry smile in his face. Death definitely comes in many shapes, but this one was a painful end to the Saint.

Loneliness is neither the swamp of vices nor the grave of life. Rather it is life itself when it uncovers its ugly face. This was the Saint's life. It was moulded by the satanic side of life as loneliness and driven by grief. A thousand Pharaohs hunted him, and he had no Moses.

Contact

Ali Hussain Al-Ridha

Al-Ahsa, Saudi Arabia

PO Box 51076

Postal Code: Al-Ahsa 31982

Email: Sirali12@gmail.com

Printed in the United States
By Bookmasters